Pun
Enchanted
Evenings

Pun Enchanted Evenings:

A Treasury of Wit, Wisdom, Chuckles, and Belly Laughs for Language Lovers

746 Original Word Plays

By David R. Yale
The Pundit of Double Entendres

A Healthy Relationship Press LLC

New York

Cover art by Katrina Joyner, http://spearcarrier.daportfolio.com.

Interior design by Imago Press, ljoiner@dakotacom.net

In memory of my Uncle, Arthur Gordon,
who told me my first (and second, third, fourth…) pun –
and got me hooked for life.

INTRODUCTION

Puns are like direct mail. Although most people secretly like them, they claim they don't. How many times have you told a really good pun, only to have the listeners groan? But then, moments later, you overhear them passing it on!

But you — and every other pun lover — can take heart! Although it's considered good form in some circles to groan at even the best puns, a recent study in the *Journal of Sighchology* by Professor Al Gerian, suggests that pun lovers share some admirable personality characteristics!

Responses to puns reflect some very deep-seated psychological traits, Professor Gerian explains. His study identifies three basic responses to puns — and their underlying personality types:

- No acknowledgement, or a nonverbal dismissal, like a shrug, indicates an extremely rigid person who thinks along straight lines and is very literal. This personality type has no imagination, minimal verbal and creative abilities, and may actually fail to understand the pun because of limited linguistic skill.

- A groan or verbal dismissal indicates a more flexible personality type with more advanced verbal skills who wants to think non-linearly, but has a hard time doing so. This personality type tends to be insecure and un-giving, and extremely fearful of change. These people may find the playfulness inherent in puns upsetting to their sense of established rules and order. Or they may actually be jealous of the punster's linguistic skills, but unwilling to admit it.

- A broad grin, a hardy laugh, or positive verbal acknowledgement is a highly reliable indicator of top-notch verbal and creative skills, and an ability to look at things from more than one perspective. This personality type is secure, generous, highly innovative, able to admire the punster's linguistic ability — and capable of responding in kind.

Building on Professor Gerian's pioneering work, Professor Sue Crohse, in a study published in the *Journal of Ego and Ideology* looked at punning as a tool for conducting job interviews. Professor Crohse found that 98.4% of the job applicants hired who laughed or smiled at puns had positive performance evaluations during the next three years. But only 32.6% of the groaners performed positively in the same period. Professor Crohse predicts that a pun response test will become a standard component of employment interviews by the year 2020. Of course if you're a pun lover you've probably suspected this all along.

Like other language lovers, you're probably curious about how I selected the puns for this book — and why I left out others. The truth is, there are a number of truly great puns I wanted to include in this book, but I couldn't — because much as I'd like to claim credit for them, I didn't make them up. All 746 puns here are Yale originals! Or at least I think they are! Great minds think alike, and it's possible someone else has come up with a few of these word plays, too.

Sure I was tempted by those all-time favorites created by the greatest punster ever, Anne Ohnimous. And there are even some blue-ribbon winners told to me by friends and family that enticed me.

Remember the story about Benny? One day in the woods, a witch appeared, told him to grow a beard and never shave, and he'd have everything he wanted in life. But if he ever cut off that beard, the witch insisted, she'd take revenge on him. He grew the beard. And he got everything he wanted. But then, after many years, his wife insisted he had to shave. Benny, always wanting to please, shaved off his beard — and was immediately turned into an urn. The moral of the story is: a Benny shaved is a Benny urned! My Uncle Arthur told me that one when I was 8 years old.

Of course you must remember that the greatest feat of strength ever performed was Wheeling West Virginia, but do you know why ant-eaters never get sick? It's because of all the little anti-bodies they have inside! My friend Judith Lukin told me that one.

Do you know where Saddam Hussein was just before we caught him? Copywriter extraordinaire Debra Krinick insists he was caught between Iraq and a hard place! And do you know what to call a regal Russian ruler who is over-scheduled? My wife Marge claims he's a biz-czar!

I still laugh out loud every time I tell the one about the difference between a beer parlor and an elephant's fart: one's a bar room, and the other's a bah-rrrooom!

Then there's the one about the Greek guy who goes into a tailor shop with a pair of torn breeches. "Eumenides?" he asks. "Yeah! Why?" the tailor says. "Euripides?" I think my cousin Billy actually made that up when we were kids.

But I've kept my temptation under control, because you've probably heard them already. And I wanted to bring you a corn-o-copia of brand new, original linguistic treats, enough for many Pun Enchanted Evenings!

1.   Did you hear about the mysterious epidemic among railroad engineers back in the 1960s? All of a sudden they had no libido. It was a really Erie Lackawanna!

2.   Why will you get a fine if you spray DDT over a bird sanctuary?
     Because that's an ill eagle activity!

3.   It rained so much back in the summer of '28 that the low-lying fields flooded, and millions of ducks flew in from everywhere, it seemed. They ate so much grain, it threatened the farmers with ruin. So the county agent decided to offer a bounty on ducks. At the meeting he called to explain his offer, one of the farmers asked if they had to send in the whole duck. "No," said the agent. "Just send the bill."

4.   What would you call a nasty remark by a Russian despot?
     Czarcastic!

5.   What did Emperor Nero's chief bill collector say to his anxious new assistant?
     "Relax! Rome wasn't billed in a day!"

6.   What would you call a Warsaw resident who holds up wires for a living?
     A telephone Pole!

7.   What would you call a really tiny apartment that you have to buy to live in?
     A condo-minimum!

8. Did you hear about the lumberjack who sold logs to the New York Central?
    He claimed he had ties to the railroad!

9. What would you call an anti-theft device at a stationery store?
    A pad lock!

10. What's the difference between a zealous crusader and an anti-water pill
    One says "die, heretic!" and the other's a diuretic!

11. What would you call a bunch of painters who are against everything?
    Con artists!

12. What would a long-haired man named Matthew do if somebody stole his bed?
    He'd sleep on his Matt tresses!

13. What would Bugs Bunny say if he were an electrician?
    "Watts up, Doc?"

14. What would you call a very flexible group of musicians?
    A rubber band!

15. What would you call an insect with a lot of answers?
    A consult-ant!

16. How did the Israeli army unit know that God was on their side when they weren't sure where the enemy was?
    The Lord said "Here, Oh Israel!"

17. Why does the mayor of an Arizona city have to be a funny man if he wants to be civic-minded?
Because he has to have a sense of Yuma.

18. What would you call the closely guarded laws of energy developed by physicists who are blood relatives?
The family joules

19. What would you call a medieval armored courier?
A mail man.

20. What would you call a very fat kept man skipping down the street?
A jiggle-o!

21. Why is writing a tweet like writing poetry?
Because you have to get your words' worth!

22. Why is an Eastern European knight in armor like a poor excuse?
Because the Czech is in the mail!

23. What would you call a thin Irish lady named Kathy?
Kath O'Lean!

24. What would you call a sophisticated verbal attack by Guerillas in India?
A punjab!

25. What's the opposite of Manhasset?
Woman has risen!

26. What's the opposite of a bag lady?
A Baghdad!

27. What do you call a verbose, close-knit group of weight watchers?
A diettribe!

28. What do you call a sad dog that loves fruit?
A melon collie!

29. What did the shipping clerk at the hearing aid company say to the irate customer who hadn't received his order yet?
"I'm going to box your ears right now!"

30. What would you call somebody who steals office supplies?
A clipto-maniac!

31. How do they answer the phone in a Mexican ice factory?
"Hielo!"

32. Why would a man named Nick Cooper sound like an astronomer when he's angry?
Because he'll shout a Cooper, Nick cuss!

33. What would you call a lock that keeps a meddling city government in Florida from getting at your personal records?
Tampa proof!

34. Did you hear about the baker who pushed his wife into the cake mix?
She claimed she was a battered woman!

35. "Now look, son. You're too hot-blooded," the old man said. "You'll have to cool down before I agree to leave you my fortune!"
"But pop! How can I do that?"
"Buy an heir conditioner!"

36. There was this Roman trash hauler in the old days, when they were clearing the swamps, who was accused of polluting the air by burning the reeds rather than composting them. What did he say to rebut the charge?
"All loads reed to loam!"

37. What would you call a joke about a light bulb?
A lampoon!

38. What would you call a female doctor who specializes in private parts?
A gal-necologist!

39. What would you call ready-made potatoes?
Pre-pared!

40. What would you call clams that won't spoil when kept at the grocer's for months?
Shelf fish!

41. Why do winning poker players seem unhealthy?
Because they look flushed!

42. When the climate changed, and the river dried up, the city wasn't a port anymore. Why did they call the media for help?
     Because they needed re-porters!

43. What would you call a person worshipped by a famous screen actress?
     A Demi God

44. Why will the followers of a famous German philosopher never be able to change their beliefs?
     Because every time they do, they re-Kant!

45. What would you do if you lost your way in a forest of fruit trees, and darkness was approaching?
     I'd sleep on the apri-cots.

46. "But I wanted two wash basins in that bathroom, the woman said.
     "Oh, I guess it didn't sink in," the plumber answered."

47. What would you call a famous pianist if he spontaneously spoke during a performance?
     Ad-liberace!

48. Why is a tired criminal likely to stay that way?
     He doesn't want to get a-rested!

49. What would you call the Sauce Chef's assistant?
     The saucerer's apprentice!

50. Why are raucous crows always righteous?
     They have good caws!

51. What would you call a foreclosed shopping center with promise?
     Re-storeable!

52. Why isn't a hard worker patriotic?
     Because his efforts are un-flagging!

53. What would you call the source of excellent wine grapes?
     De vine!

54. What would you drink if you want to catch a cold?
     A cup of cough-ee!

55. What kind of work does the publicist for x-rated films do?
     Pubic relations!

56. What would you call somebody in the middle of a hip operation?
     Uninhipited!

57. What did the Rain God say to his apprentice on his birthday?
     "Today you can dew whatever you want!"

58. What would you call a campaign to introduce metric weights?
     A pro gram!

59. What would you call a guide to the guests at a small
    hotel?
    An inn-dex!

60. If a pen company and a light bulb manufacturer merged,
    where would it locate?
    Pen-sylvania!

61. What game do ducks play?
    Wing toss!

62. What would you call a French immigrant with kids who
    now lives in Genesee County and says he doesn't know
    anything?
    Je ne sais pas!

63. What would you call a positive outlook on middle age?
    Forty-tude!

64. What would you call a low-octane Irish fuel?
    Gas O'lean!

65. What would you call someone who tries to suppress a
    book about Hollywood in the name of patriotism?
    A star-spangled banner!

66. What bodily mechanism tells you to go to the
    bathroom?
    Urinate sense!

67. What would you call it when a man runs off with a mail
    order bride?
    Env-elope!

68. What would you call a narcissistic sea creature?
Self fish!

69. What do baggage handlers and social workers have in common?
They both complain that their case loads are too high!

70. What's the difference between a bull's bellow and a matador?
One's audi-bull and the other's awed the bull!

71. What would you call a heated philosophical argument between two residents of Warsaw?
A Pole-emic!

72. When should your feet go to confession?
When they're wearing mocca-sins!

73. What would you call contentious poems by a Latin American insurgent?
Contra-versey!

74. What would you call an unreasonable demand by a very mischievous person?
An imp-osition!

75. The boarding house had fallen on hard times, and everyone in town was afraid that if it didn't get some new boarders soon, Old Mrs. Smithers would have to close it. So they were all excited when word went around that a new tenant had shown up. But alas, it was an unfounded roomer!

76. Why can't Ella and Samuel marry?
Because their kids would be sick with Sam 'n' Ella!

77. If a person could get gasoline just by being grateful, how would they feel?
Tankfull!

78. What would you call a beggar in the largest city in France?
A Parisite!

79. How did the fisherman know he'd landed a record-breaker?
He looked at the scales!

80. Do you like tropical fruits?
Bah! Nah!, Nah!

81. What would you call a machine that made solid fuel out of soda pop?
A coca coaler!

82. What would you call an over-qualified housekeeper doing the last step of the laundry?
Ironing bored!

83. What would you call an Eastern European butter substitute?
Magyar-ine!

84. What tree never grows crooked?
A plumb tree!

85. What would you call the stock-in-trade of a gambling supply house?
Merchan-dice!

86. What would you call a long list of comedians?
A card file!

87. How did one spring flower greet the other?
"Hiya, Cynth!

88. Why do prospectors go crazy when someone steals their ore?
Because they've lost their mined!

89. What did Tom McGee say to the priest about his promotion at work?
"Quia facit McGeehi magna!"

90. What's the difference between a Japanese car and a rocking horse?
One's a Toyota and the other's a toy oater.

91. What would you call a very heavy soup?
Won ton!

92. First the Boston City Council raised the greens fee on the public golf courses yearly. Then they did it every six months. Golfers were furious. But after the Council raised it again in May and June, the golfers broke down the fence and played without paying. What did they call it?
The Boston tee party!

93. What kind of snacks do ducks like best?
Quacker Jacks!

94. What would you call it when a spectator punches a member of the visiting soccer team?
A fan belt!

95. What would you call the process of thinking up double entendres?
Pundering!

96. What would you call a western state after a particularly bad drought?
Aridzona

97. Why are so many pool players deaf?
They clean their ears with cue tips!

98. Why can't a famous boxer be a real hero?
Because every win shows you a feat of Clay!

99. Why didn't Saddam Hussein treat Iraqui minorities better?
Because it never OKurd to him!

100. Why doesn't Annette J. Sering pick up her phone when it rings?
Because she has an Anne Sering machine!

101. What would you call an offer of services to the Police Department by an informer named Bill?
The William tell overture.

102. What would you call a book about male sex organs?
A dick-tionary!

103. What would you call a man wearing a codpiece?
Naddily dressed!

104. What would you call the instruction book for a computer program that calculates interest rates on credit cards?
The Userer's Manual!

105. What would you call a suntan gotten on horseback at a high altitude?
A Mount Tan!

106. Why did Giovanni and Manuela Roffone's baby cry so loudly?
Because his name was Mike Roffone!

107. Why did the ocean liner fall apart when the shipping line fired all its employees?
Because they took away all the ship'screws!

108. Why did the sailor cut off a big branch from a tree growing on the beach?
Because he wanted to be sure he would have many shore leaves!

109. What major war could have been set off by idle wordplay?
The Punic war!

110. What would you call a night club where the fiddle music is really awful?
A vile inn!

111. What would you call the constant pressures and problems faced by a park manager on the Canadian border?
Niagravations!

112. What would you call a British lady arsonist?
A charwoman!

113. What would you call a certified 50 year old bottle of fine Beaujolais?
Genuwine!

114. The American tourist staying at a bed and breakfast inn in the English countryside asked the innkeeper about the purpose of the large ceramic pot under the bed. "Oh, that!" the innkeeper replied. "We use that in loo of a toilet!"

115. Why wouldn't the Armenian government issue a birth certificate to Hagop and Kallia Gerian's newborn son Albert?
Because they said he was an Al Gerian!

116. What would you call a well-known TV hostess if she became an advocate of an Eastern religion?
Nirvanna White!

117. There was a famous Jungian analyst named Springtime, who was known as the most devoted Jungian disciple. But then one day, a new analyst came to town who was even more devoted. What did they sing to him? "Junger than Springtime, are you!"

118. What can you drink to excess, and still walk upright? Plumb wine!

119. What would you call a particularly persuasive and charming anti-war advocate? Disarming!

120. What do they eat with turkey in Australia? Canberra Sauce!

121. Why is the shipping clerk with protective hand gear on sure to be a champion? Because he has his boxing gloves on!

122. Why did the army officer always crack corny jokes? Because he was a kernel!

123. What would you call a bungling baker? The muffin' man!

124. What would you call an evergreen tree that grows at high altitudes in Europe? An alp pine!

125. What would you call a protest rally by evil spirits? A demon-stration!

126. Why was Rosetta Zankowitz's fiancee especially optimistic?
Because he knew he had a Rose Z. future!

127. What would you call a very fast merry-go-round?
Whirled class!

128. What would you call a place that sells pillories and restraints?
A stock and bond market!

129. Why didn't the boaters get wet when the boat capsized?
They were playing bridge!

130. What language do bridge builders speak?
Span-ish!

131. What would you call a kiss from someone who speaks with a forked tongue?
A masokiss!

132. Back in the old days, what did they call the famous ball park after a rain, when the worms emerged from the sod?
Wriggly Field!

133. What would you call a mint-flavored drink that makes people insane?
Creme d'mented!

134. What would you be if your nephew was a carburetor?
A carb-uncle!

135. What would a train wreck do to the ridership on a
     commuter railroad?
     Detracked from it!

136. What would you call a river that was so polluted it
     couldn't flow?
     Ill liquid!

137. What would you call a collection of propaganda books?
     A lie-brary!

138. What would you call a mushroom that reproduces
     irregularly?
     Spore-adic!

139. What would you call a tropical flowering bush that says
     nasty things in the night?
     A hibis-cuss!

140. What would you call a multicolored doorway?
     Varie-gated!

141. What's another name for a dirty picture?
     X-pose-ure!

142. Why did the moron dress in paper bags?
     He wanted to wear sack cloth as a sign of penitence!

143. "The sofa you sold me is junk," growled the angry
     customer.
     "I wouldn't couch it in those terms," answered the
     salesman.

144. What would you call an intensive body building course for flabby people held on Saturday and Sunday?
Weakenders!

145. What would you call a desire to drink an ocean of lemon-lime soda?
A Fanta® sea!

146. What would you call a sleight-of-hand performed by an actor or actress?
A theatrick!

147. What would you call a wooden mug for a hot Chinese drink?
A teak cup!

148. What would you get if you question the right insect?
An antswer!

149. Why do electricians love to leave home in the morning?
Because they get a charge out of their work!

150. Why are bakers always aristocratic?
Because they like to loaf and they're well bread!

151. What would you call a medication for autistic felines?
A catatonic!

152. What kind of stunts would a very old magician perform?
Geriatricks!

153. For years, bird meat was sold as a delicacy by Australian butchers, loose and by the pound. But then one day an American marketing hotshot decided to package it with a big, fancy label. Why?
Because he decided to take a brand gnu approach to marketing it!

154. "Daddy, would you believe Mommy made spaghetti for dinner again!"
"I wouldn't put it pasta!"

155. What did Putin say to the security chief of one of the republics when there was a danger of rebellion in the grasslands?
"Better watch your steppe!"

156. When the moron found out his house was too big and he couldn't afford to heat it anymore, what did he do?
He hired a contracter!

157. How does a New Yorker fix a car without tools?
With a tawk wrench!

158. What did the animal trainer say when asked if he could teach a big, majestic bird to swim?
"I think I can fin-eagle it!"

159. Why would a foot fetishist be regarded as deeply religious in Japan?
Because he's a shin-toe-ist!

160. What would you call trying to squeeze a size 15 butt into size 9 pants?
Ass-a-nine!

161. Why can't a ticklish person wear eyeglasses?
Because the spec-tickles would be too much for him!

162. Why wouldn't the senator accept the lobbyist's gift of a leather jacket?
His constituents would know he was suede!

163. What would you call an uncompromising, but courteous, male rider of mass transit?
Intransi-gent!

164. What would you call an x-rated version of making beautiful music together?
Concerto for two organs!

165. Why did the moron freeze very small insects and put them in the radiator of his car in very cold weather?
Because he was low on ant-i-freeze!

166. Why is a woman named Celia Juss who lives in a canyon, beautiful no matter what she looks like?
Because she's always gorge Juss!

167. Why does the weather change after a glacier retreats?
Because there's moraine!

168. Why must you use a pencil to draw a level line?
Because if you use a pen, you get an ink line!

169. Why is it so expensive to surgically re-connect a dog's tail?
Because you pay re-tail!

170. Why shouldn't you eat a Chinese dish made from pig's feet?
Because you might get toe-mein poisoning!

171. What would you call a passion for renaming Parisian streets after those in Bucharest?
Rue mania!

172. What would you call a clandestine lovemaking session between two shrinks?
A psychia-tryst!

173. Why did the moron throw stones at the big black birds in his yard every February?
Because he wanted crow cusses!

174. What would you call the results of an underwater knitting class for oysters?
Purls!

175. Why would insults from a man named Al seem strange and foreign to Americans?
Because they're Al jeers!

176. What's the difference between the cause of discomfort on a hot summer day and spontaneous singing?
One's humidity, and the other is hum a ditty!

177. What instrument should you use to play decadent music?
A disso-lute!

178. Why did the moron hit an egg with his axe?
He wanted to see if he could hatchet!

179. What would you call an employment agency run by Mr. Handel that specializes in cafeteria workers?
Handel's Mess Hire!

180. Why can't you agree with your spouse about absolutely everything today?
Because that would be "Yes, dear! Day!

181. How can a small creature swell to many times its normal size after sucking your blood?
Because it's an elastick!

182. What would you call petty disagreements among the workers at a pen company?
Bic-ering!

183. What would you call someone who really pursues her death wish?
Deadicated!

184. Why does a man who makes word jokes have a strong aroma?
Because he's a pun gent!

185. Why is someone who skips school like an insect?
Because he's a true ant!

186. What would you call a person who automatically gives you advice every time your pet barks?
Dogmatic!

187. Why does the baker's assistant always feel so deprived?
Because he kneads dough so much!

188. How did the famous Spanish guitarist burn his hands?
     He played flame-enco!

189. Why could Hamilton Humbert Illick never be knighted?
     Because he would become Sir Illick and lose his British
     nationality!

190. Why are bakers seldom tall?
     Because they always work with shortening!

191. What do you call the part of the beach where the waves
     break?
     The surf-ace!

192. What does a pharmaceutical salesman named Samuel
     carry?
     A Sam pill case!

193. What would you call a polluted fog that leaves a fine
     layer of dust after it dries?
     A resi-dew!

194. What would you call a gambler's heaven?
     Pairadice!

195. Why will a group of singing instructors be concerned
     with the homeless?
     Because they're the how sing authority!

196. Why is breeding rabbits so scary?
     Because it's hare-raising!

197. What would you call a pilgrim who travels to a holy city without feeling anything?
Mecca-nistic!

198. Why does a secret marriage between insects turn them into a mammal?
Because it's an ant-elope!

199. What's the difference between a reticent woman named Nola and shoe polish?
One's a shy Nola, and the other's Shinola®!

200. What would you call an excellent natural flavoring for broth?
Soup herb!

201. Why did Monica's mother look for sharp edges on her daughter's new musical instrument?
Because she didn't want it to harm Monica!

202. Why does a fashion photographer work more quickly lying down?
Because he's already re-posing!

203. What's a good nickname for a songwriter named Richard?
Lyrick!

204. What would you call an Israeli woman who drives a car from Scandinavia?
A Saabra!

205. Why don't Roto-Rooter men like to go out at night?
Because they always come home feeling drained.

206. Why might a woman named Jean feel unclean?
Because everyone always says "Hi, Jean!" to her!

207. What would you call it if a publisher flooded the market with dozens of new books?
A title wave!

208. Why are fishermen so rhythmic?
Because they cast a net!

209. What drink could keep you from getting ahead?
Pover tea!

210. What would you call a quickie in the back seat?
A Chevro lay!

211. What medication do you give a pig with laryngitis?
Oinkment!

212. Why do people laugh when a knight is angry?
Because Sir cusses are funny!

213. Why is a sick dog named Warren like a hare's home?
Because he's a rabid warren!

214. Why can't you let an inconsistent man named Wayne polish floors?
Because sometimes he waxes and sometimes he Waynes!

215. What would you call an ordinary French greeting?
A common allez-vous!

216. What would you say when you arrive late at your mother-in-law's house if the only way to get there is by sliding on your butt down a five-mile-long, snow-covered hill?
"It tuchus a long time to get here!"

217. What should you say when a good friend starts a new printing business?
Words of ink-couragement!

218. What would you call music composed in a washroom?
Sink-opated!

219. What would you call the best serf on the manor?
A champ peon!

220. The director of manufacturing sent a memo to the engineering department asking them to change the specifications on some new products to eliminate production problems. But engineering refused. The director stormed into the chief engineer's office and said "What's this?? I don't get no re-specked?!"

221. What would you call moving a famous performance center to a new location by truck?
A Carnegie haul!

222. What would you call the warm-up exercises for a competitive walking event?
The pre-amble!

223. What would you call a plan full of mistakes?
A blooperint!

224. What should you say when you're tickling a yuppie's baby?
"Gucci, gucci, koo!"

225. Why do political campaigns do so well in the spring?
Because of all the leaflets on the trees!

226. What would you call a change in position by a dogmatic political party that has nothing to do with the facts?
Amending the Party Lyin'!

227. What did the townspeople say to the prospector who just rode in from the desert by horseback after 6 months of successfully prospecting for gold without a single bath?
"You reek, uh!!"

228. Why is a cuspidor musical?
Because it's a spit-tune!

229. What's the difference between a drugstore and a shrimp farm?
One's a pharmacy, and with the other, you farm a sea!

230. What would you call a washroom on Mt. St. Helens when it's erupting?
A lava-tory!

231. What's another name for a gymnasium?
A body building!

232. Which tropical bird causes most forest fires?
The flame-ingo!

233. Why are carpenters so good at giving advice in difficult times?
Because they have plenty of coping saws!

234. How did the unarmed prisoner in the Stalag in a cave overcome ten guards and gain his freedom?
He hit them with a stalag might!

235. What would you call an armed conflict between the prophetesses in ancient Greece?
A Sybil war!

236. Why did Wayne wear only a sweater in the bitter cold of winter?
Because Wainscot was too heavy!

237. Why is an ale truck with broken springs very literary?
Because it Shakespeare!

238. What would you call a country where everybody worries a lot?
A constern nation!

239. What would you say about a Mexican teenager who stole a train?
He must have had a real loco motive!

240. What would you call a trade journal for hangmen?
A nooseletter!

241. Where would you buy a soup-making machine?
     In the souper market!

242. What would you call a quick sketch of an Arctic bird?
     A pencilguin!

243. What did the shrink say to the patient who was afraid he
     was flipping out?
     You can deep end on me!

244. What would you call a put-down by your boss?
     A mana-jeer!

245. Why is making love to a romance novelist as boring as a
     city in New Jersey?
     Because when it comes right down to it, it's hack in sack!

246. What would you call fancy foods from a South
     American country?
     Peruviands!

247. What would you call too much impractical book-
     learning?
     Wis-dumb!

248. Why don't sign painters like to make corrections?
     Because they really need their jobs and they don't want
     to re-sign!

249. Why wouldn't a fancy store re-package famous perfume
     in small, trial-size containers?
     They wouldn't want to be re-vialed!

250. What would you call a husky female truck driver named Kim?
     Kim Burly!

251. What would you call a 16-year-old who likes to follow schedules?
     A rou-teenager!

252. What would you call someone who studies audible signs of weariness?
     A sigh-cologist!

253. Why didn't Indian canoes last long?
     Because the owners were always disembarking!

254. If you were a baker, what would you say about a rumor that your bread was poisoned?
     "Taint so!"

255. Why shouldn't an avid chess player marry someone from Prague?
     Because she'd always face a Czech-mate!

256. Why do people get particularly crazy if their stoves are repossessed?
     Because they become deranged!

257. What would you call a country where everybody is trained to kill?
     An assassin nation!

258. Why wouldn't a 1950's baker drive one of those funny-looking cars with the airplane-type nose?
Because if it crashed and burned, it might have stewed the baker!

259. What happens if you swallow Easter egg colors?
You get in-dye-gestion!

260. How can a flower avoid being eaten?
By shooting its pistils!

261. What would you call a square-dance caller's wages?
Dosi-dough!

262. Why does an unsuccessful dowser look ill?
Because she's not feeling well!

263. Why is it so easy to fool birds at the beach?
Because they're so gull-ible!

264. What would you call a resident of Bangor who says crazy and reckless things?
A Maine-iac!

265. Why is a recently mortgaged mine like a Southern delta city?
Because it's got New Ore Liens!

266. Why won't some cats wear mittens?
They're afraid they'll get claws-trophobia!

267. Why did Donald the billionaire go to a music store to look for a wife?
He was looking for a Trump-ette!

268. What's the leading cause of divorce in long-term marriages?
A stale mate!

269. Why did the railroads have rigid regulations for allocating sleeping space on old-time overnight trains?
They felt berth control was very important!

270. What would you call a mirage of a roadblock?
An obstacle illusion!

271. What would you call a famed cowboy with a digestive spasm?
Wild Bill Hiccup!

272. What do you get when someone whacks your car with a 3-pronged tool?
A tri-dent!

273. What would you call a long, thin, brilliantly colored, voracious fish with wavy patterns on its sides?
A moiré eel!

274. Back in Victorian times, when pale women were considered beautiful, they used to go to the beauty pallor!

275. What would you call the best clam chowder in New England?
Souperior!

276. Why is it risky to build a very long double-decked bridge?
Because the span decks will stretch too much!

277. Why did the moron take several swings at the street light with his axe?
He wanted big lamp chops!

278. What would you call an Eastern European offset printer named Wayne?
A litho-waynian!

279. What would you call an electrically-grown fruit?
An ampear!

280. What would you do if you were out in the woods and the sky was falling?
I'd gather up cater-pillars to support it!

281. What did the father say to his son who didn't want to learn fractions?
"You half to do it!

282. Why did the moron put his melodeon out in the yard?
He wanted to do organic gardening!

283. What's another name for a grass trimmer?
A mow-chine!

284. And then there was the lady with too many suitors. She sprinkled soap powder around her house because she thought it would deter gents!

285. How can a flower avoid being eaten?
By petalling away fast!

286. What would you call an Irish coconut cookie?
     A MacAroon!

287. What could you say about the threat of submarine warfare?
     It has a sub stance to it!

288. Why are the songs surveyors sing while working so mundane?
     Because they're plat etudes!

289. What would you call a particularly bad forecast of your future?
     A horror-scope!

290. What would you call the ultimate design for an efficient fig orchard?
     The best con-fig-uration!

291. Why might a recent immigrant from Asia become confused?
     Because he's dis-oriented!

292. What kind of insects make you feel really secure?
     Insure-ants!

293. What's another word for cutting down a tree?
     Trunk-ating it!

294. Who is the patron saint of machinery?
     Saint Pawl!

295. Why did the debate team captain start to quote proverbs when her team gained the lead?
Because she wanted to maxim-ize her advantage!

296. Why can't Louise Staeke get anything right?
Because she's Miss Staeke!

297. How do we know that Hungarians are democratic at heart?
Because they believe in Magyar-ity rule!

298. How can a sentry keep from being bored?
By reading the magazine of his gun!

299. Why did his colleagues laugh when the plant breeder announced a new variety of Harrhar Tree that survives northern winters?
Because it was a hardy Harrhar!

300. What would you call the understudy to a French horn player?
A substi-toot!

301. Why do actors and actresses like to appear on Broadway so much?
Because of the Big Apple-ause!

302. What would you call a British politician who likes to wash a lot?
A lava Tory!

303. What's the difference between a pre-schooler and a graduate student?
One uses play dough and the other studies Plato!

304. What kind of formal legal documents would be drawn up by a lawyer named Margaret?
Marga-writs!

305. During a fiscal crisis, a large Northeastern city put up toll gates on its main street, Belle Boulevard. During the next fiscal crisis, things got so bad, the city sold the Boulevard, compete with the gates, to a private operator. But the mayor refused to give the public any information about the arrangement. Now nobody knows for whom the Belle tolls!

306. Julius Caesar Domenisco was an inventor with a patent on a process for brewing beer and wine. But then someone else developed a better way, and as brewers converted, he lost a lot of royalty income. When his best friend converted, he said "Et tu brew thus?"

307. What would you call a religious Israeli with a caustic sense of humor?
An acidic Jew!

308. How do shepherds find their way across the trackless wilderness?
By the lambmarks!

309. What would you call a Middle Eastern writing instrument?
An Arab-bic!

310. Why should you never step near Currant bushes?
You don't want to get caught in the under Currant!

311. How does a farmer feel when his hay crop fails?
      Dis-strawed!

312. Why does a rhythmic, ticking sound surround an
      Alaskan city?
      Because it's Metro Nome!

313. Why does a wig worn in a play seem to be living?
      Because it's an act-tress!

314. Why did the moron put a nail in his front yard to ward
      off thieves?
      He heard that a tack is the best defense!

315. What would you think about a potion that turns people
      into cats?
      I don't know, but it would give me paws!

316. Why do residents of a New Hampshire town grow peach
      trees in every available nook and cranny?
      They want everything to be peachy Keene!

317. Why is a lazy farm wife named Ida likely to migrate to
      the Rocky Mountains?
      Because her husband is always saying "Ida, hoe!"

318. What would you call an effort to limit the growth of an
      Australian city?
      Perth control!

319. What would you call a smile that covers embarrassment?
      A cha-grin!

320. Why can't a man named Russ stalk deer?
Because no matter how carefully he moves, there's
always a Russell!

321. Why is a woman named Fran like a California city after
she breaks up with her boyfriend Cisco?
Because she's Fran sans Cisco!

322. Why would a waterfowl driving a Chrysler-built car be
unlikely to have an accident?
Because it's a duck 'n Dodge!

323. What would you call a rhyme you make up to encourage
yourself when you're looking for a place for the car?
A parking meter!

324. What would you call a news program on a really dull
day?
A snoozecast!

325. Why do miners sneak off to read adventure stories on
the job?
Because their work is so boring!

326. Why can't a famous amusement park ride be made out
of wood?
Because then it wouldn't be a ferrous wheel!

327. What would you call it if you got a bunch of pennies in
your change, all with the same date on them?
A coin-cidence!

328. What would you call it if your husband orders your dessert at a French restaurant without consulting you?
A parfait accompli!

329. What would you call it if the mob muscled in on a soup kitchen and insisted on mixing the ingredients?
A gang stir!

330. What did the cop say to the excuse made by the joy-riding teenager who drove over an embankment and landed in the branches of a huge oak tree?
"You're parking up the wrong tree!"

331. Why would bringing an art museum guide along insure a successful hunt?
Because the docent will attract big bucks!

332. How should you dress to ward off cholera?
With choler stays in your shirt!

333. What would you call an avant-garde sculpture made with cream of wheat instead of papier-mâché?
Cerealistic!

334. What do you call it when your most valuable player takes a bathroom break?
A champ peein'!

335. What kind of clientele do you have if you suddenly cut your quality of service?
Cuss-tomers!

336. What can you say to someone who is making a pest of herself trying to convert you to Orthodox Judaism?
"Who says that Yahweh is better than my way?"

337. What meter should affirmative poetry about writing instruments be in?
I-am-bic!

338. What's the difference between drinking a toast and faking an accident claim?
One calls for champagne and the other for sham pain!

339. What did the driver of the overloaded truck say when the state trooper told him to drive onto the scale?
"I can't go on this weigh!"

340. Why did the Missouri cabinet-maker step across the state line when he had some complex curves to cut?
He wanted to use an arcin' saw!

341. What's the difference between the mistress of the manor at a summer party and one of her servants?
One wears a lawn dress, and the other is a laundress!

342. Why do masochists blink a lot?
They want to give themselves eye lashes!

343. Why is a person who makes lots of excuses an advocate for a dairy product?
Because he always says "But!... err!..."

344. What would you call a feminist candy?
A Her-she bar!

345. What would you call someone who was just pretending to be mischievous?
An imp-oster!

346. Why did the moron mix mint in the souffle?
Because he was eggspearaminting!

347. Why is a compulsive investor like a sweet pastry?
Because they're both dough nuts!

348. What would you call a symphonic piece that uses unusual amounts of percussion to depict the strife of post-modern life?
Cymbolic!

349. Why is Sandra Schiff always in trouble?
Because her name is Miss Schiff!

350. Why did the chef quit when the restaurant owner insisted he over-spice the food?
He felt he was wasting his thyme!

351. What would you call a form of Eastern European currency issued only on Fridays?
A pay Czech!

352. Which Middle Eastern politician was quoted most?
Anwar Said dat!

353. Why is a man who keeps a woman always tense?
Because he has miss stress!

354. Why does Deanna Jones' boyfriend feel like a movie star whenever they make love?
Because he's in Deanna Jones!

355. Why is a misguided man named Samuel really a powerful warrior?
Because he's Sam awry!

356. What kind of cereal do uncouth people eat?
Oafmeal!

357. Why is camping during rainy weather so memorable?
Because it's a very in tents experience!

358. What would you call sisterly competition between ancient Greek prophetesses?
Sybiling rivalry!

359. Why did the office supplier lose his biggest account?
Because he padded the bill!

360. What would you call a marketing campaign for a bond issue to build more correctional institutions?
A jail sell!

361. What would you call a joint condition caused by excessive practicing of the 'cello?
Sympho-knee!

362. What do you get if you take too much antacid?
Symptums!

363. What would you do if the captain of the ship you're on is about to back into a restricted area?
Give him a stern warning!

364. Why is an idyllic California city like a bunch of Christmas elves?
Because it's Santa Crews!

365. Why did the railroads have so much trouble with steam engines?
Because they were always running hot and coaled!

366. If your big toe has a sore spot, how can you plant a tree with your bare foot?
Stick your ache corn in the ground!

367. What would you call a plan to raise money by turning the steeple of a church into a bed and breakfast?
Inn spired!

368. How would you attempt to hide facial expression of your emotions?
Neutral eyes them!

369. What would you call a speech by a mine owner exhorting his workers to produce more?
An ore-ation!

370. Why do comedians get fat?
Because they in jest so much!

371. What's the most important thing when you're sewing a design on a dress using shiny ornaments?
Getting them in the right sequins!

372. What disease does a boarding house owner get when she has problem tenants? Roomertism!

373. What's the perfect name for a door-to-door saleswoman?
Isabelle Wringer!

374. Why did the old-time lumberjacks, who sang while they used two-man saws, have to know trigonometry?
Because they used logger rhythms!

375. Why was Caine's brother such an easy victim?
Because he wasn't Abel to defend himself!

376. Why shouldn't you put a baby's dirty diapers in the laundry bin?
You wouldn't want to hamper his movements!

377. When the artisan finished the sundial in the wealthy musician's garden in ancient Greece, his client thought it was too plain, and needed a frame or border. "How about some rock around the clock," the artisan asked!

378. Which tropical islands are havens for insects?
The Ant hillies!

379. What would you call an arrogant driver of a large vehicle?
Truckulent!

380. What would you call a pet bird with just enough training to do the job?
A para-keet!

381. Why did the moron want to be a toucan?
Because he thought toucan live cheaper than one!

382. What do philosophers take when they're feeling run down?
Pla-tonic!

383. Did you hear about the guaranteed fishing worms? If you don't catch anything, you get a re-bait!

384. Why did the moron call AAA when his yard was suddenly over-run with hopping creatures?
He wanted to have them toad away!

385. Why should you be careful when you tease a man named Russell?
Because when he's angry, he's danger-russ!

386. Why will it provoke a fight if an optician always uses smelly glass to make lenses?
Because he'll be vile lens prone!

387. What would you call somebody who tinkers with the ventilating device under the roof several times a day?
An attic fan-atic!

388. What would you do if a dozen of your horses broke loose and were wandering along the County Road?
I'd try to stable-ize the situation!

389. Why can't a queen dressed in her royal garments get wet in a drenching downpour?
She's wearing her reign coat!

390. Why do map makers concentrate on mountain peaks?
Because they're into top-ography!

391. How can you power a huge locomotive with batteries?
If they're D cells!

392. What would you call a proposal to sun-dry a bumper crop of grapes to keep them from spoiling?
Raisin-able!

393. Why would someone named Sal, who likes Edgar Allan Poe's works, ask so many women to marry him?
Because he's a pro-Poe Sal!

394. Why does Stanislav Dorf's goldfish prefer to live alone?
Because he's a Stan Dorf fish!

395. Why is a nurse named Kathleen Smith so fond of dispensing pills?
Because she's Medic Kate!

396. Why is a gentleman farmer who grows a pickling herb so meticulous?
Because he's a dill-igent!

397. Why won't the florist talk about his plans for decorating the harvest ball?
Because mum's the word!

398. Why is an inarticulate woman named Margaret like an old-fashioned American boys' game?
Because she's mumble-t-peg!

399. Why did ancient Germanic warriors attract swarms of flies around their legs?
Because they had Hun knees!

400. Why should you never get uptight about sleeping outside in the wilderness?
Because if you get tense, you can always sleep inside one of them!

401. What would you call an impudent and deadly verbal attack?
A sassination!

402. During the wars in ancient Greece, when the City was attacked, the young woman jumped into a huge pottery vessel. Undetected by the soldiers, she was the only one to survive the invasion. She said ever afterwards that her life was Owed to a Grecian urn!

403. What would you call the formal structure of Mozart's "A Musical Joke"?
Har-har-harmony!

404. Why do high-yielding cherry trees need so much water?
Because they drupe a lot!

405. Why did the teenager misunderstand his father's intent when he broke up with his girlfriend, Joyce?
Because his dad said "Re-Joyce!"

406. Why doesn't Monika's mother need a nickname?
Because she already has a Monika!

407. Why did the moron go around the city letting air out of tires?
Because he wanted to counter inflation!

408. What do herding dogs grow in their gardens?
Collie flowers.

409. Why did the pathologically hyper woman have her nails done every day?
She was hoping for a manic cure.

410. What would you call a government agency designed to track down illicit tinkering and inventing?
Device squad!

411. What would you call the attitude that there's no hope in this world because religious laws are continually being broken?
Sin-acism!

412. What kinds of words do mathematicians like best?
Add-verbs and add-jectives!

413. What kind of food does a bad comedian eat?
Corn meal!

414. Why did the moron fall down the stairs?
He was wearing slip-pers!

415. What would you call a flowering bush that likes to take root in the cracks in asphalt or cement?
A Road-odendron!

416. What happens when a crazy wallflower grows old?
He becomes a wallnut!

417. What did the pea say to her sister?
"Howdy, podner!"

418. When the contractor had great difficulty installing the custom-made and very expensive stained glass windows in the church, he groaned all night. "What's the matter, honey?" his wife asked him. He answered "Oh! I have terrible window pains!"

419. What would you call a library of rare spices?
The ar-chives!

420. What would you call a poem about a fixture on a workbench?
Vice-versa!

421. What's the perfect nickname for a woman named Bettina who likes cereal for breakfast?
Wheat Tina!

422. What would you call an Italian structure with adjustable sides used for hunting ducks that live along the canals?
A Venetian blind!

423. What would you call an undersized Belgian ant?
An Antwerp!

424. Why do Scandinavians make such lovely furniture?
Because they know all about the Finnish!

425. Why is a shiny fire engine like a loaf of dark bread?
Because it has lots of pumper nickel!

426. Why did the relatives of a famous German poet start a brewery?
Because they were Heine-kin!

427. What would you call a famous New York hotel, surrounded by fences during its reconstruction?
The walled-off Astoria!

428. What was the nickname of a very scholarly medieval composer?
"Books" Tehude!

429. How do you make a sheep sexy?
Sheer it!

430. What would you call it if Queen Katherine gave up her throne?
Abdi-Kate-ion!

431. What would you call an unusually confident piece of sales promotion?
A bro-sure!

432. What would you call a magazine about famous young
      birds?
      Peeple!

433. What would you call someone who is forced to listen
      to a long-winded and very dull lecture about making
      preserves?
      A jam-boree!

434. Did you hear about Jerzy Urban, the former spokesman
      for the Polish Communist Party? He became a capitalist,
      migrated to the U.S. and changed his name to Jersey
      City!

435. What would you call an illness you get every few
      months?
      Sicklical

436. When the employment agency advertised exciting
      jobs available at the World's Fair, but then tried to get
      applicants to work as ditch diggers at the local landfill,
      what were they accused of?
      Un-Fair labor practices!

437. What's the proper attire for a Board Meeting?
      A lumber jacket!

438. What would you call the entrance to an inquisition?
      An interro-gate!

439. What would you say about a person who's very good at
      composing religious music?
      She has a great hymnagination!

440. What does a frustrated sadist organizer sing?
     I can't get no sadist-faction!

441. Why would Amy's whining husband make a good
     cannon?
     Because he's always saying "Aim meee!"

442. What would you call a speckled spud?
     A spotato!

443. What would you call a dry cleaner who's meticulous
     about removing stains?
     A fuss spot!

444. What would you call Indian money found in a bog?
     Swampum!

445. What would you call a boss who insists on choosing
     your wallpaper for you?
     Patternalistic!

446. Why shouldn't a truly religious person wear sackcloth?
     Because it's sackreligious!

447. What would you call a pastry served at an Indian
     concert?
     A ragamuffin!

448. What would you call a vast improvement in antacids?
     A quant-tum leap!

449. Why does it make sense to have disgusting dirt in the
     corners of a hunting lodge?
     Because it's lodge ick!

450. What would you call the results of a fender-bender caused by a beginning driver?
A stu-dent!

451. What would you call a very large device for shooting arrows?
A jumbow!

452. What would you call the pasta served at a fashionable resort?
Spa ghetti!

453. What would you call it if a swarm of bees slapped you in the face?
Bees' wacks!

454. What's the difference between an illegal Scottish cap and a small fowl?
One's a banned tam and the other's a bantam!

455. Why did the British army officer live in the bathroom?
Because he was a loo-tenant!

456. What did the lawyer say when the county sought legal action to ban skinny-dipping at the nudist colony?
That will be some swim suit!

457. Why did the moron think he owned the place after he got 25 cents interest on his savings account?
Because he had a quarter interest in the bank!

458. How did Ralph on the Honeymooners get his last name?
He lived in a tiny apartment before he was married, and he was really crammed in!

459. What happens if you hit a beaver at high speed?
You get a ro-dent in your car!

460. What would you call a self-stick, textured wall surfacing material?
Tac-tile!

461. I like Alaskan cities, Juneau what I mean?

462. What regulation would a dictator pass to make sure he had ultimate control over everybody in his country?
A rule of thumb!

463. What would you call an overnight stay in a bad part of town by rich, chic people seeking a new thrill?
A slum-ber party!

464. What do Minnesotans say after a 23 inch blizzard?
"'Snow big deal!"

465. And then there was the retiree who liked to bake because it kept him occu-pied!

466. Why is the king of beasts the laziest animal?
Because he's always lion around all day!

467. Why is it perfectly fare for a fashion designer to break an agreement with his competitors and make a sudden, dramatic change to his winter line?
Because he's a turnstyle!

468. Why do men want to kiss women on the first date?
Because they think it's the quick-kiss way to get what they want!

469. During the boom days there was a terrible shortage of office supplies and they got very expensive and had to be carefully rationed. It got so bad you had to pay per clip!

470. What's the difference between tall trees in Kansas and someone who's just eaten Yankee Bean soup?
Nothing! They'll both break wind!

471. Why did the moron refuse to eat in the doctor's reception area
He wanted to cut down on his weight and get seen faster!

472. Why was the inventor of the cannon doomed?
Because he immediately became cannon father!

473. Why were the Japanese so unwilling to try Western-style furniture?
They were very chairy of it!

474. What would you call two days away with a lady named Lee during which you realize you're crazy about her?
A love Lee weekend!

475. Why is an iron lion who likes to ski so fierce?
Because he's ferro-shuss!

476. What would you do if the lights went out in a spice store?
I'd light the canned dill!

477. Why did the moron tie up his dinner guests?
He wanted to give them a cord-ial welcome!

478. What would you call an attack on the quality of a
     restaurant's French fries by a food critic?
     A frying pan!

479. Where would you go to learn how to write comedy?
     Ham line college in St. Paul!

480. Why can't Harold Astor Luce drink alcohol?
     Because he'll get Hal-Luce-inations!

481. Why is a badly made Yuletide drink like an x-rated
     movie?
     Because it's the result of poor nography!

482. Why is it so hard to make money selling dirty jokes?
     Because it's a very risqué business!

483. What would you call a treasury of silly jokes?
     A corn-o-copia!

484. What would you call a royal personage on a tour of
     Venice?
     King of the rowed!

485. Why would a baseball buff with indigestion want to own
     Babe Ruth's ghost?
     Because then he could have a fan tum!

486. Why is a pile of wet turkey manure so incomprehensible?
     Because it's gobble-de-gook!

487. The seamstress, captured by an invading army, knew
that the ruthless king was very fond of gathered curtains,
but nobody in his kingdom knew how to make them.
What did she do when she was brought before him?
She pleated for mercy!

488. What would you call a medieval sex manual?
Sex and the Single Churl!

489. How would you feel if a knight in shining armor rode up
on a white horse, announced you'd won $1,000,000.00,
and handed you a check?
I'd be pleasantly sir prized!

490. What would you call a cap worn by a singing French taxi
driver?
A cab beret!

491. Why did John Locke's laundress want to marry a nut?
Because she was a Locke washer!

492. Did you hear about the Hispanic guy who had an
identity crisis? He drank soy sauce and it went away!

493. Why might you make a lot of errors after eating tainted
canned greenbeans?
Because you've got botch-ulism!

494. What did the minister of war say to the King who
wanted an offensive consisting strictly of knights?
"Your majesty, there'll be a sir charge for that!"

495. Why are people who grow hay so devoted to their farms?
Because it's the fodder land!

496. Why did Sonny Bono's wife leave him?
Perhaps because he didn't Cher-ish her enough!

497. Why do taxidermists use glass eyes?
Because most people don't real eyes they're fake!

498. What's the difference between a fake bull and a real bull in a China shop?
One's a sham bull and the other makes a shambles!

499. How would you feel if a thief stole all your clothing, belts and ties?
I'd be dis-appointed!

500. Why can't you drive to the town of Waycross?
Because no matter how close you get, it's still Waycross Georgia!

501. Why are women attracted to a man who figures on his fingers?
Because he's a hand summer man!

502. Back in the drought years of '33 and '34, the price of spices and herbs shot way up, and most people did without them. But Giovanni knew that Italian food must be spiced, and his restaurant's future depended on finding a way to pay for proper seasonings. So he took out a bank loan to pay for them. All his friends said he was living on borrowed thyme!

503. Why would an accountant be so good at raising fruit?
Because he's good with fig years!

504. How can you be sure the waterfowl on your doorstep are foreign?
Because they're porch-a-geese!

505. What would you call the daily small talk among people who remove stones from cherries?
Pitter patter!

506. What would you call a young woman who really knows her geography?
An atlass!

507. Why is a powerful mentor in the business world like a spectator sport?
Because he's a jai-alai!

508. Why are Midwesterners so religious?
Because they live on the prayer-ie!

509. What would you call it if someone drove their small truck through your herb field?
Van-dill-ism!

510. What would you call it if they paved over an entire Greek island?
Con-Crete!

511. Why is a hen that strays from the nest like a Sartre play?
Because there's no eggs sit!

512. Why would a hypnotic weight reduction process where you repeat the word "lean" cause high blood pressure?
Because it's a "say lean" solution!

513. Why was Sam Molive's father always squeaky clean?
Because he was Pa Molive!

514. Why doesn't an inventory clerk at a beverage warehouse drink whiskey?
Because he's a tea totaller!

515. Why would you put a herd of cows on the radio?
If you wanted mooed music!

516. What's the difference between a common dinner dish and a competition for goof-offs?
One's a meat loaf and the other's a loaf meet!

517. Why do bankers always walk around with peach pits in their mouths?
Because all they want to do is suck seed!

518. What's the leading communications problem in the business world today?
Too many memorandumbs!

519. What would you call the meeting place of fat cat politicians?
The rotund-a!

520. What would you call a hound after it's run through a thicket?
A burred dog!

521. Why can't Mr. & Mrs. Falsa sell their fine custom-made mattresses under their own name?
They could be sued for Falsa rest!

522. What should Sam and Harriet Littikl name their daughter, who they want to be a world-renowned psychologist?
Anna!

523. What's the difference between a container for plants and a box for lottery tickets?
One's a window box and the other's a win dough box!

524. What would be the most important qualification for a lyric writer for Bic® pens?
A pen-chant for the job!

525. In what country do they write lots of dark and brooding romantic verses?
Poe-land!

526. Why do soldiers seem so relaxed after they buy things at the store on base?
Because it's the calm-issary!

527. Why would you search for a sea lion's nest before going on a cruise?
To be sure you have your seal eggs first!

528. What kind of exercises can you do with just a pen?
Aero-bic!

529. What kind of raw materials do you use to build underwater nuclear-powered boats?
Sub atomic particles!

530. Why would you never name a boy Victor Timothy?
Because then he'd always be the Vic Tim!

531. What spice gives Hungarians a strong sense of self-identity?
Magyar-om!

532. What would you call a stubborn old metalworker who makes food and water containers by hand?
Can-tank-erous!

533. What do you get when you ferment a barrel of nickels and dimes?
Coin-treau!

534. Why can't you believe you'll have a future with a beautiful woman named Fay?
Because she's a Fay belle!

535. What did the supermarket manager say when his employee told him that hundreds of mice were making the customers scream?
Don't tell me store-eeee's!

536. What kind of clothing should a chimney-sweep wear?
Something soot-able!

537. What would you call a game of cards based on words?
Ling-whist!

538. What would you call someone who is unconsciously cold and impersonal?
Frig-id!

539. What would you call a gargantuan quantity of stewed chicken?
A fricas-sea!

540. Why are the people leaving a particular Greek island forever so smelly?
Because they're all ex-Crete-ing!

541. What would you call a linguistic study of Julius Caeser's last words?
Et tu mology!

542. Why are size "E" brogans more valuable than others?
Because they're boot E!

543. Why is swatting stinging insects so musical?
Because it's bee bopping!

544. What's the difference between a small, cramped building and an illicit container?
One's a band box and the other's a banned box!

545. What chemical would you use to etch parallel lines in pen barrels?
A-score-bic acid!

546. What would you call a splinter group of priests who believe that charitable works are the church's most important mission?
A bene-faction!

547. What would you say if the Pillsbury Dough Boy played baseball?
Batter up!

548. What would you be if someone claimed they were selling you wine made from a tall, woody grass — but it was only colored water?
Bamboozled!

549. What would you call an idyllic, beautiful country full of hostile people!
Angri-La!

550. Why would a masochist want to make "beautiful music" with a sadist named Gertrude?
Because she's a hurty-Gerty!

551. What would you call a cash register at a comedy club?
A chortill!

552. What would you call the thoughts of a dirty old man?
Codger-tations!

553. What would you call it when your tele-transmitted document gets garbled?
A faxident!

554. What's another name for mood music?
Mellowdies!

555. What would you call it when a woman gooses her boyfriend for the first time?
A test tickle!

556. Did you hear why the new rehabilitation program that teaches embroidery to prisoners failed?
They consider it crewel and unusual punishment!

557. Why did the moron always show his girlfriend to the exit?
He wanted her to know he a-doored her!

558. What would you say to the spiritual leader who helped you through a night of grief?
Good mourning!

559. What would you call a revolutionary who always wears white, wrinkled clothing?
A Marxist-Linenist!

560. Why is it more efficient to have a large team of singing surveyors?
Because things go better when you have a plat tune!

561. What kind of undergarment would a mathematically-inclined mermaid wear?
An algae bra!

562. What person with supernatural powers would you call to get rid of a growth under your skin?
An exorcyst!

563. Why do gourmet chefs especially value Nash Brand cookware?
Because they can cook with pan Nash!

564. Why might a 40's big band have played very slowly and sounded like it was under water?
Because the leader was Lawrence Whelk!

565. What would you call a secret apology from one telegraph operator to another?
Remorse code!

566. Why is a flavorless after-dinner mint like words of praise?
Because they're both blandish mints!

567. What special decoration do soldiers hang up at Christmas time?
Missile toe!

568. What would Julius Caeser say if he invaded Gaul using a high-speed modern jet?
"I came. I saw. I Concorde!"

569. Why did the moron take candy to the car dealer?
He heard new cars cost a mint!

570. What would you call a wind so strong it could blow your work surface away?
Desk-gusting!

571. What's the difference between a mythical creature and a fib told by a woman named Laura?
One's a Lorelei and the other's a Laura lie!

572. What's the difference between a thick Soviet newspaper and someone's overly-generous posterior?
One's a fat Tass and the other's a fat ass!

573. How can you send a gift of linens by phone?
     With a flax machine!

574. Why is a boarding house resident named Nathan always
     so preoccupied?
     Because he's roomin' Nathan!

575. Why is Mr. Trump so funny when he tries to dodge
     reporters?
     Because he does the Donald duck!

576. If you were the CEO of a large food-processing company,
     how would you respond to the charge that frozen baked
     goods aren't as good as fresh?
     "It ain't nece-sara-lee so!

577. Why is a messy woman named Christine usually in a
     festive mood?
     Because she's always creating a Chris-muss!

578. What's the difference between a detached, calculating
     man and a woman strutting her stuff?
     One's a cool operator and the other's a culotte parader!

579. Why would a fish that swallowed a children's game be
     very artistic?
     Because it would be jacks in pollock!

580. Why would a utopian author try to write with a sharp
     tool?
     Because she wants everything to be awl write!

581. Why is a caveman's door like an English monument?
Because it has a stone hinge!

582. How would you know when you're hiring a truly
dedicated taxi driver?
When he says that it's his favorite hacktivity!

583. What would a teenager get if she steals an expensive,
feather-filled overcoat?
A good dressing down!

584. What would you call a young male insect who swindles
you with flair and style?
A flim-flam-boy-ant!

585. Why can't Richard Vant be knighted?
Because he'd always be a Sir Vant!

586. Mark Smith is always flattering his boss, Mr. Brett. What
could you say about Mark?
He knows what side his Brett is buttered on!

587. How could a man named Matthew keep from going bald
by sheer will power?
Mind over Matt hair!

588. What would you call a loud, wild, public display of
lovemaking by two giant bears in a zoo?
Panda-moanium!

589. What would you call a prank where young boys throw
each other in an Egyptian river?
Juve-Nile!

590. In a land where men rule in splendor for one day, but spend the rest of their lives at hard labor, what would you call the ex-monarchs?
Were king class!

591. What would you call an angry, hostile spouse who tries to annihilate you?
A deci-mate!

592. What would you call a musical composition where you have to play the harp with your feet?
A concertoe!

593. What would you call it if your feet fell asleep and stayed that way for months?
Coma-toes!

594. What would a claustrophobic flea say?
"Let me out of hair!"

595. What kind of flowers never grow on hilltops?
Dale Lilies!

596. What would you call the warning device in a car you steer with your feet?
A shoe horn!

597. Why are deli countermen inherently nasty when they talk about their work?
Because they're always making cold cutting remarks!

598. Why will a new college town be the capitol of the universe?
Because it will be called Universe City!

599. What do you get when a streetcar depot burns?
Car barn dioxide!

600. Why will a pretty Parisian street make you sick?
Because it's the Rue Belle-eh!

601. Why is the rind of a Martian soup fruit like a kangaroo?
Because it's a Mars Soup Peel!

602. Why do the Scotts like tar beach so much?
Because they can get free tar tans there!

603. Why should a soup kitchen with a huge, manually-stirred pot have a truck driver on staff?
Because one person can't stir it alone, so you need a team stir!

604. Why do archery instructors repeat themselves so much?
Because they're teaching taut-ology!

605. Why doesn't Jason Portman need a suitcase?
Because he packs everything in his Portman toe!

606. Why is a crow's charge for singing like a beverage?
Because it's a caw fee!

607. Why is the fourth hilltop a good place to find food?
Because it's the four ridge place!

608. Do you like Western pine trees?
      They don't grow near me so I have no o- piñon!

609. What would you call a supply of heavy oil reserved for
      making acrylic false teeth for draft animals?
      Ox-i-dental petroleum!

610. What destination sign do army draftees want to see on a
      bus?
      Not in service!

611. What would you call a car that carries its offspring in a
      little pocket?
      A Subaroo!

612. What would have happened to Pharaoh's army if God
      had parted a major river instead of the Red Sea?
      It would have been a-Nile-ated!

613. If a woman had to choose between 3 serious suitors, each
      named Nicholas, why would it be easy?
      Because it would be a pick Nick!

614. What would you call it when small birds refurbish their
      homes?
      Wrenovations!

615. What would you say if your tennis opponent says you're
      playing a lousy game when he's losing?
      The pall is in *your* court!

616. What would you call a Middle Eastern cloth likeness of
      an animal that you keep in your auto?
      A Persian car pet!

617. How would you cross a deep, wide river just by drawing on your mental powers?
I'd use my attention span!

618. Why would a little girl named Estella Maria Ramirez excel at everything she does?
Because she always gives a 'stelle R. performance!

619. Why is someone who can smell a winning hand like a popular mountain resort area?
Because she has a poker nose!

620. What would you call a watch maker who is so fussy, even the sound has to be right?
Met-tick-ulous!

621. Why shouldn't you put together a high-powered sun tanning machine from a kit?
Because if it malfunctions, you'd be a real bask kit case!

622. Why did Attila's battalions inspire so much terror?
Because it wasn't a simple fear, it was a Hun dread!

623. What's the difference between factories that make I beams and corn whiskey?
One's a steel mill and the other's a meal still!

624. What's the difference between a gardening center and a bunch of thieves?
One sells fences and the other fences when it sells!

625. By what look can you tell a religious fanatic?
Moral eyes!

626. What would you call an animated after-dinner confection that makes nasty, cruel word-plays?
A punnish mint!

627. What would you call a particularly dumb but very forceful statement?
Ass-sertive!

628. What would you call it when an expert plants grass to try to make the desert green?
A pro-seed-ure!

629. Why wouldn't a blue-jay name his son Jacob?
Because birds have fledgelings, not jay cubs!

630. Why didn't cowboys like to work on Jim Trubb's ranch?
Because Jim's cattle were nothing but Trubb bulls!

631. How can you objectively measure someone's sense of self?
With an am-meter!

632. What would you call a woman who sometimes laughs and sometimes gets really discouraged by a man's dirty habits?
A man ick depressive!

633. Why is a male prostitute inherently effeminate?
Because he's a fee male!

634. Why could you go blind at a fat farm?
Because you couldn't see any thin!

635. What would you call it if a poet started writing novels?
De-versifying!

636. What would you call a song about the male ruler of a Middle Eastern beehive?
The Sheik of Arab bee!

637. Why is it hard to digest your food when you have double-thick jeans on?
Because you're wearing your duo-denim!

638. What would you call a shipping clerk in a candy factory who can't keep track of the after-dinner mints?
Mint tally deficient!

639. What mental exercise could you use to make it easier to have a tooth extracted?
Transcend-dental meditation!

640. What would you call a place where they leave dog sleds overnight?
A barking lot!

641. Cowboy Bill had been warned to never mess with the Dillo gang. But when Tom Dillo swooped down out of the hills, all by his lonesome, Cowboy Bill figured he had a chance. So Cowboy Bill lashed out at Dillo with his trusty 50 foot bullwhip. But Dillo seemed to have armored skin, the whip had no effect, and the poor cowboy got shot up something fierce. What did his boss say about it?
"I told him never to try to disarm a Dillo!"

642. Why can't you get an electrician to change a fuse?
Because when he agrees, he re-fuses!

643. What would you say about someone who boarded a
flight from Helsinki and disappeared?
They vanished into Finnair!

644. What would you call a large building with distinctive
architecture used for a circulating library?
A lendmark!

645. What sign should the owner of an upscale apparel store
put in his window at night?
Clothed for business!

646. What's the difference between a specialized doctor and a
greeting card writer?
Nothing. They're both cardiologists!

647. What musical instrument would help along
disarmament talks?
An accord-ion!

648. Why is a very old elephant like a city in Alabama?
Because it's tusks are loose-ah!

649. Why did the moron freeze small insects and put them in
the radiator of his car in very hot weather?
Because he was low on cool-ant!

650. Why does an indecisive artisan have supernatural
powers?
Because she's deciding which craft to do!

651. What would you call a quartet of singing cats?
Mew-sicians!

652. What would you call a rock 'n' roll song about a story-book elephant that suddenly saw a mouse?
Babar ran!

653. Why is a huge bunion on Samantha Greene's left big toe like a canned vegetable?
Because it's a Greene giant corn!

654. Why do celebrities get running noses and watery eyes when autograph hounds converge on them?
Because it's a sign us attack!

655. What would you call it if you took away a gun from someone dressed up as an after-dinner candy at a masquerade party?
Disarm a mint!

656. What would you do if you were afraid of attacks by arsonists?
Paint my house char truce!

657. What would you call an unexplained reaction in the laboratory?
A chemystery!

658. Why did Vincent change his name?
Because of inflation. Now it's Vindollar!

659. Why do doll makers always have money?
Because all they have to do is get together on the up elevator, and they've raised a bunch of doll-ers!

660. Why do very young residents of Warsaw look like baby frogs?
Because they're tad Poles!

661. What would you call a splinter group of environmentalists who were paid off to minimalize the importance of foul industrial smells?
The putre-faction!

662. Why does a gristmill look like it's covered by fungus on summer mornings?
Because of all the mill dew on it!

663. Why is Elizabeth V. Lee's sewing like an Israeli city?
Because it's a Beth Lee hem!

664. What's a nickname for a woman named Kathleen who gives as much as she receives?
Recripro-Kate!

665. How would a disorderly, untidy man named Hugh turn barren land into fertile fields?
Because he's always creating Hugh muss!

666. Why is a teenager so scary after he gains six inches?
Because he grew some!

667. What would you call an analogy in a tele-transmitted poem?
A fax simile!

668. Why is beer a good medicine?
Because it's good for what ales you!

669. Why don't people like wash basins set at floor level?
Because they don't like to sink so low!

670. What would you call informal clothing suitable for every place you go?
Any wear!

671. Why are dogs imprecise?
Because they are afraid to be de-tailed!

672. What would you call a counterfeiting ring in a historic Pennsylvania town?
The Valley Forgery!

673. Why does Leo dance in the door whenever he's late?
Because he's Leo tardy!

674. Why can't William Loew go outside in a hurricane?
Because a strong gust could send him Bill Loewing away!

675. Why is a young snake ambitious?
Because it has asp irations!

676. Why will you get an electric response if you tease Jennifer when she's angry
Because you'll make Jen irater!

677. What would you call it if you could grow blueprints on a farm?
A plan-tation!

678. Why did the moron prefer cheap quilts?
Because he thought he'd only have to pay 10% down!

679. Why do corn syrup salesmen always look for amusement parks?
Because they're hoping for a huge Karo® sell!

680. Why can't an innkeeper become overly reliant on his hostelry?
Because even when he does, he's an inn dependent person!

681. Why would a very funny comedy about a beer-maker cause a major controversy?
The audience reaction would be a brew ha-ha!

682. What would you call an oversupply of knights in armor?
A Sir plus!

683. Why is a Cockney draft animal named Theodore, who suddenly changed into a man, always tired?
Because he's ex 'orse Ted!

684. What would you call a computer program that helps authors write strange supernatural tales?
A weird processor!

685. Why don't illegal fisherman have to cook their catch?
Because it's already poached!

686. Why didn't the founder of Pennsylvania have to worry about retirement?
Because he already had a Penn chin!

687. How would you feel if you were invited to dinner at
Millicent and Hugh Smith's house, but they had already
dined when you arrived?
Hugh, Millie ated!

688. Why would a cross between a worthless mongrel dog
and a small insect be edible?
Because it's a cur-ant!

689. What's the difference between a rancorous divorce and a
person with an out-of-style haircut?
Nothing! They both parted on the wrong side!

690. How do get rid of an old clunker?
Plant car away seeds!

691. Why is ignoring an artic bird like a distress sale?
Because it's an auk shun!

692. Why can't coffee shops get good counter help these days?
Because when it becomes efficient, it's counter-
productive!

693. In what part of the New York metro area do all the
gardeners live?
Lawn Guy Land!

694. What would you call a solid gold percussion instrument?
A status cymbal!

695. Why can't you put a rare cookie in a bank vault?
Because it would be a safe cracker!

696. What would you call a person who studies community-oriented insects that live under ground?
An ant-ropologist!

697. The moron planned to sell building lots in the arctic circle after global warming melted the polar ice cap. Why did his scheme fail?
Because it wasn't well thawed through!

698. Why is Swiss cheese so healthy?
Because it's hole-some!

699. What did the census supervisor say to the employee who went on an unauthorized vacation?
"Have you taken leave of your census?"

700. What would you call scalp exercises to prevent baldness?
Hairobics!

701. Why must somebody whose very identity is tied into the beach live in Southern California?
Because she has a sandy ego!

702. Why are people who like to dance to Brazilian tunes so dour?
Because they're often in a Samba mood!

703. Why can't Milos and Marya Urgic name their son Albert?
Because he'd be Al Urgic to most people!

704. If 10 killer bees were after you, and you managed to swat just one of them, why would you be out of danger?
Because then they'd be nine!

705. What kind of ham does the National Rifle Association prefer?
Pro shooto!

706. Why are people who use nothing but candles so puritanical?
Because they see everything in a wicked light!

707. Why couldn't the smuggler produce any money even though he had bundles of large bills belted to his body?
Because he was really strapped for cash!

708. Why is a baker's dozen such a strange concept?
Because it dozen't add up right!

709. Why is an expression of affection in the back room of a store that sells cold cuts so special?
Because it's a deli kissy!

710. What's the difference between a lithograph and the writing of contract clauses designed to take the customer's rights away?
One's a fine art print and the other's the art of fine print!

711. What would you call a short story about a rivalry between chemists and physicists at the Argonne National Laboratory?
Science friction!

712. What's the perfect name for a woman who advocates that unemployed people should cancel their mortgages?
Burn-a-debt!

713. What would you call a main dish made of ground meat and a little sugar?
Sweetish meatballs!

714. Why do mill workers who make colored wood talk so much?
Because their work involves a lot of dye-a-log!

715. Why is Katherine such a people pleaser?
Because when she was young, her overbearing mother always commanded "Play, Kate!"

716. Why don't two mischievous people do well as couples?
Because they're imp paired!

717. Why are people who yearn for honey-making insects so wealthy?
Because they have plenty of bee longings!

718. What did the old man say when he finally found his false teeth?
"I can't live without chew!"

719. Why don't Tums® work for certain six-legged insects?
Because they're ant acids!

720. Why does the small enclosed area at the top of houses in an Italian city always smell so good?
Because it's a Rome attic!

721. Why is Augustus Mastropietro always so serious?
Because he doesn't want to be considered a fun Gus!

722. What do you get if a matador falls in the olive press?
Oil of olé!

723. How did Boris Yeltsin get one of the largest Communist news organizations to support him?
He kicked Tass!

724. Why don't matadors get hurt often?
Because they're very cape a bull!

725. Why is Roy's grandson like a less expensive pair of dress trousers?
Because he's only a quarter Roy!

726. Why would a salvation-minded sinner with a lisp want to marry a hirsute woman named Grace Jones?
Because she'd be his shaving Grace!

727. What's the difference between a corrupt cop with a guilty conscience and his honest counterpart?
One feels awful and the other feels lawful!

728. What would you call an awful community choral group that everybody's ashamed of?
Embarras Sing!

729. What award would a woman get for a principled avoidance of members of the opposite sex?
Honorable men shun!

730. What would you call an overweight Mexican revolutionary?
Pauncho Villa!

731. How would you convince women to buy genuine leather handbags?
By purse sueding them!

732. If a teenaged girl ignored her mother's warning and got a terribly painful sunburn, what would her mother say?
"That should be a less sun for you, young lady!"

733. Did you hear about the beggar who heard that the richest man in the world would be walking down his street? He spent days figuring out how to ask the rich man for a lot of money, and went hungry because he neglected his other begging. Finally, the big day came, and he approached the rich man, but he was turned down. The moral of the story is "don't put all your begs in one ask it!"

734. Why is a sleeping pill for cattle so powerful?
Because it's a bull dozer!

735. What might a religious fanatic utter to further the cause?
Moral lies!

736. A man who lived in rural Ireland had to get his wife to the hospital in a hurry, and a storm had washed out all the river crossings. Why wasn't he worried?
Because her name was Bridge-it!

737. The former premier of the USSR became homeless after he lost his job. He lived in the streets of Moscow, and became an expert at scrounging food in the dumps, and cooking gourmet meals with it. What did they call him?
Garbage Chef!

738. Why did early computer designers avoid the binary number system?
Because they thought it was un-ten-able!

739. What would you call a square pen?
Cu-bic!

740. Why do poets make good comedians?
Because they're always a-musing!

741. What would you do if you were a personnel manager and there was a shortage of research scientists?
Plant a chemist tree!

742. Why is a man named Hugh always doing abrupt about-faces?
Because even a small change in direction is a Hugh turn!

743. What would you call a very shy insect?
A reluct-ant!

744. Why are the smallest components of a Honda so musical?
Because they're Accord-ions!

745. Why is someone who eats three loaves of a popular white bread so special?
Because he's Wonder Full!

746. What do you need to publish an eBook of puns?
The right eQuip-ment!

AUTHOR'S NOTE

I Hope You Really Love This Book!

Thank you for buying and reading *Pun Enchanted Evenings*. I hope you enjoyed many good belly laughs!

I'd love to hear your reactions, comments, praise, criticisms, and anything else you have to say. Please email me at David@bestpuns.com.

If you really love this book, please help spread the word! Here's how you can help tell the world about *Pun Enchanted Evenings*:

1. Tell your friends, and wheedle, cajole, and inveigle them to buy their own copies of the eBook version at https://www.smashwords.com/books/view/9425, or the paper version at www.bestpuns.com/buy1. If they're not ready to buy, tell them to follow us on Twitter @bestpuns, where they'll get a regular flow of enchanted puns from this book.

2. Ask your local library to order a copy. Please give them the ISBN number for the paper version: ISBN 978-0-9791766-4-7, and the url: www.bestpuns.com/buy1.

3. Link to www.bestpuns.com on your website. You may quote up to 10 Yale puns on your website, providing credit is given to *Pun Enchanted Evenings* by David R. Yale and www.bestpuns.com.

4. Write a review of *Pun Enchanted Evenings* on Amazon.com, Amazon.ca, Amazon.co.uk, or for your favorite website or print publication.

Thank you for all you do.

—David R. Yale

Original Puns Wanted!

If you have original puns of your own, and you'd like to see them in print, you've come to the right place! A Healthy Relationship Press LLC will be publishing *The World's Best Puns* in 2011, and you can submit yours for consideration. For more information, go to www.bestpuns.com/world.

About the Author

David R. Yale has had short stories published in *Midstream*, *Response*, and *Jewish Braille Review*. The *Front Room*, one of his short stories, won an Award in a *Writers Digest* Contest. He has read from his fiction at Union College (Schenectady NY), Claremont College (California), The University of Minnesota, The Mendota (Minnesota) Jazz Emporium, and UCLA.

Yale's anti-porn novel, *Saying No to Naked Women*, includes a pun-cracking heroine. You can find out more about it at www.SayingNoToNakedWomen.Com. If you're into self-discovery and self-awareness, you'll enjoy *Saying No to Naked Women*.

One of Yale's nonfiction books, *The Publicity Handbook*, was a Fortune Book Club Selection. A classic in the field, it's still in print 28 years after publication. For more information, please visit www.PublicityHandbook.com.

Yale studied fiction with Grace Paley at the Juniper Institute of the University of Massachusetts as well as with Joe Caldwell at the 92nd Street Y. He holds a B.A. from City College of New York and an M.A. from the University of Minnesota.

Yale, an international direct marketing consultant, lives in New York with his wife and daughter.

Follow David Yale on Twitter!

For additional copies, or your favorite Yale puns on T-shirts and coffee mugs, go to www.bestpuns.com/buy1. You'll also find links to buy e-Book versions there. You can follow Yale on Twitter @bestpuns.